# THE STRUGGLES OF CAREGIVING
## 28 Days of Prayer

Nell E. Noonan

UPPER ROOM BOOKS®
NASHVILLE

LIBRARY OF CONGRESS CATALOGING-IN-PUBLICATION DATA
Noonan, Nell E.
  The struggles of caregiving / Nell E. Noonan.
    p. cm.— (28 days of prayer)
  ISBN 978-0-8358-1091-3
  1. Caregivers—Prayers and devotions. 2. Bible—Devotional use. I. Title.
  BV4910.9.N665 2012
  242'.4—dc23                                         2011044202

# CONTENTS

# ACKNOWLEDGMENTS

On Saturday mornings I attend Fort Worth Writers where we critique, advise, and share our wordsmith calling. The group comprises published authors, writing teachers, newbies, and every kind of writer in between. Week after week, month after month, they have listened to my devotions with professional skill, but, most important, they have listened with their hearts. I am eternally grateful for their encouragement and support.

I would be remiss if I did not also acknowledge the contributions to my writing and my spiritual life made by an experienced caregiver, my spiritual director, the Right Reverend Sam Hulsey.

The journey my husband, Bob, and I are on would be so difficult without the generous support and constant acts of compassion made to us through the years by the clergy, staff, and our church family at St. Barnabas United Methodist Church, Arlington, Texas.

In conclusion, I thank God for Bob Noonan who shows me depths of faith and courage and for our mutual journey that stretches me to spaces of unbounded grace and love.

# INTRODUCTION

If you are reading this book, chances are you are one of the more than 65 million unpaid family caregivers in the United States. We come in a variety of relationships. Some are spouses like me, some adult children caring for parents (some long distance like me), members of the "sandwich generation" caring for their children and elderly parents, a sibling caring for another sibling, and grandparents raising grandchildren. Caregiving has become a major issue of our time with the explosion of senior baby boomers and an enormous increase in longevity of our elderly population.

Caregiving takes an enormous toll on providers. They stand at risk for a host of mental and physical illnesses, many of which have roots in exhaustion, stress, and self-neglect. They are driven by empathy, love, and devotion but often experience sadness, anger, frustration, guilt about their feelings, despair, loneliness, and depression. They need to find ways to take care of themselves and to discover beneficial coping strategies.

At an Alzheimer's Association symposium I heard Dr. Majid Fotuhi outline steps to better health and delayed memory loss for both caregivers and receivers: (1) tease your memory (brain games); (2) strengthen your heart through exercise; (3) be curious and learn; (4) laugh more often; and (5) eat smart. When this distinguished neurologist/researcher/professor finished his presentation, I wanted to shout, "But there is one more step, equally important, that was not named: pay attention to your *spiritual* health."

What has surprised me most about caregiving is that it is a cataclysmic spiritual experience. Care providers struggle with tough questions: "Why is this happening, Lord? How long must it go on? Why must our loved one suffer so? Where are you, God? Where can I find the strength to go on?" My spiritual struggles have unearthed some amazing mysteries during this odyssey. The caregiving situation teaches and blesses us along the journey. It tutors us in self-sacrificing love and forgiveness. It expands our capacity for compassion and our awareness of connectedness with all humanity. It is the ultimate response to Jesus' command to "love one another as I have loved you" (John 15:12). Caregiving asks the best of us—to love without payback, to mutually respect the spirit within ourselves and in our care receivers, to be intimately committed to someone.

The journey bumps us up against powerful negative feelings. It forces us to become more real, to ponder the meaning of our changed lives, and to struggle with issues of loss and death. And in many cases, it lasts for a long time, years and years. The biggest transformation came for me when I began to view the situation as a mutual path toward God for both caregiver and receiver. The journey turned from being a negative interference in my life to be endured into a life-giving walk filled with God-winks and enlightening lessons to learn (sometimes over and over).

Care providers have numerous tough—really tough—days. I urge you to join me in finding time for daily devotions to massage and strengthen your spirit. Time apart with God equips us to experience Love so we may not only survive but make a difference through our holy work of loving service. My prayer is that as you pause daily to listen to your life, you will come to know with certainty the Great Divine Heart loves and cares. You are not alone but walking with and toward the Holy One.

## How to Use This Book

The daily grind of providing care for a loved one is full of challenges. The book is divided into four weeks, each dealing with a category of struggles: (1) struggles with frustration and faith; (2) struggles with identity; (3) struggles with guilt; and (4) struggles to find equilibrium.

I suggest you find a place—a comfortable chair near a table—where you can keep a Bible, this workbook, and a candle and lighter. Start each session by lighting the candle to acknowledge Christ's presence. Begin your devotional time with silence. Read the scripture for the day slowly, letting the words soak into your soul. Pause for more silence. Read the life account. Reflect on what emotions or experiences surface for you. Be honest with both God and yourself as you pray. Make notes about your thoughts and feelings. Be specific.

If possible on Sundays, attend community worship. Some of you will not be able to arrange that, but all are invited to use the suggestion for deeper reflection on the week's theme found in the section "Sabbath Time."

Before each writing session for this book, I lit a candle and prayed, "Lord God, make these words more than words; make them the words of Jesus." May you hear words you need for your holy work caring for a loved one: words of comfort, strength, assurance, grace, blessing, and peace. Amen.

# WEEK 1

........................

## Struggles with Frustration and Faith

# MONDAY
## *Achy Hearts*

**Read Psalm 51:10-17.**

His skin was the color of ashes. When not napping, he fought to stay awake. My husband, Bob, began to complain about pain in his chest and down his left arm. Since it was Sunday and he suffers with numerous aches and ailments, he decided to wait and see if the pain remained the next morning before calling the doctor.

Monday, when the doctor's office opened at nine, we phoned Dr. Smith's nurse. She told us to get to the emergency room. "But I have to deliver Meals On Wheels this morning," I mumbled. She raised the volume and firmness of her voice and said, "Call them and cancel. You don't understand me. Take him to ER . . . *now*!

Tests showed an abnormality at the apex of Bob's heart. He'd had a heart attack, but not recently. His serious health problems and bent-over, twisted posture made him high risk for additional procedures to diagnose his condition, so he sat in bed to wait and see. Four days and two prescriptions later, Bob was discharged.

The day after his discharge I was scheduled to travel five hundred miles to attend my mother's ninetieth birthday celebration. Mother is more fragile, with a cancer on her eyelid and worsening circulation in her feet. I desperately wanted to be with her and my siblings. Now I could not. Once again I had to cancel sitters and stay home with Bob. Guess who had the achy heart?

For days, disappointment and despondency kept me

on the verge of tears. My anger was exacerbated by the fact that Bob seemed fine—quite chatty and perky after doctors concluded there was nothing seriously wrong. He did not even offer an "I'm sorry you missed your mother's birthday." The devilish thought that he manipulated the whole episode to keep me at home slipped into my head. I felt like my heart-room had been flooded during a dastardly storm, and when the waters receded, smelly mud and nasty gunk had seeped into every cupboard and crevice. I was snippy and avoided Bob, except for the duties of his care.

I tried to rein in my sulking attitude but could not effect change within my heart. One morning a week later, I began my daily devotions as I have for years with the plea found in Psalm 51: "Create in me a clean heart, O God." Wow, look at those words—the Lord is the one who cleans. What is impossible for me is possible for God. I simply must ask and wait on the Lord. Then God comes with flood bucket, mop, and soapy water.

## Prayer

Gracious Lord, I can talk with you honestly about

........................................................................................

........................................................................................

........................................................................................

........................................................................................

You don't chastise me for angry thoughts about my care receiver and our challenging lives. You simply roll up your sleeves, pull on your boots, and send forth saving help again. Thank you, O Lord. Amen.

# TUESDAY
## *Whatever*

**Read Isaiah 43:1-7.**

A young woman in the Bible class commented that someone told her if she had enough faith, she wouldn't have problems in her life. She wanted to know how she could get that kind of faith. Why do so many of us think being a Christian is going to guarantee an easy life? A tiny cross around your neck will not keep away a terrible diagnosis, a failure, or cruel loss. God never promised a trouble-free life. The Bible is filled with the saga of God's people facing persecution and suffering. Jesus declared, "In this world you will have trouble" (John 16:33, NCV). Notice he did not say *may*; he said you *will* have trouble. People of all faiths get sick, lose their jobs, and experience heartache and strife.

Millions find themselves hurled into the challenging world of caregiving. None of us asked for it, nor expected life to turn out like this. A friend of mine, a member of the "sandwich generation," taking care of teenage children and a parent with Alzheimer's disease, has a candid expression to sum up her experience: "It sucks." Yes, it does.

We have little choice about most of the things that go wrong in our lives, but we do have choices about how to approach them. We can insist on solitary misery and stoicism. Or we can allow God to partner us in our struggles. Our God is a God who delivers, not *from* trials and brokenness but *out* of them. With God's assistance, we get not under, over, or beneath but *through* our challenges. The cost may be everything—health, families, friends, jobs, even our lives. But letting go of control and turning to the Eternal One promises a stupendous payoff. We receive peace and fulfillment through companionship with the God who delights in being with, encouraging, loving, and saving God's children.         .

When feeling engulfed by an overwhelming situation, I sometimes recall a fictional but nonetheless moving story I received in an e-mail. After a devastating forest fire, rangers trekked around a large park assessing the damage. One ranger found a bird in the ashes, literally petrified and perched on the ground at a tree base. Sickened by the sight, he took a stick and knocked over the bird. Three tiny chicks scurried from under their dead mother's wings. She had not abandoned her young nor tried to escape the toxic smoke. The heat scorched her, but she remained steadfast, willing to die so her babies would live.

Whatever may come our way today or tomorrow, God is like the mama bird—our refuge who loves to everlasting. My new motto is "Let go. Let God. And let come (whatever it is)."

### Prayer

Loving Lord, I struggle to let you be in control. Help me

.................................................................................

.................................................................................

.................................................................................

Partner me in this journey of suffering and joy and grant me your peace. Amen.

# WEDNESDAY
## *Me and My Shadow*

**Read Psalm 17:6-8; 57:1-3.**

"You ask me how I'm doing. I'm tired . . . really tired. My mother follows me everywhere. I can't go in the bathroom or transfer the clothes from the washer to the dryer without her standing at the door watching my every move. Yesterday I mowed the lawn and as I walked back and forth with the mower, she went from the bedroom window to the sliding glass doors watching me. There are millions of frustrations in taking care of Mom, but few things irritate me more than being followed all the time. I can't get away from her." The words came from Lana, a lovely woman with a family and the additional responsibility of caring for her mother with Alzheimer's.

Other members of the support group echoed her distress. They reported that their forgetful loved ones become fretful if they disappear into the bathroom or elsewhere in the house. The care receivers constantly interrupt whenever their care providers try to rest or get their work done.

Expressing feelings in this safe setting is therapeutic. Without fail, those expressed feelings are transformed through the remarks and insights of other group members. Julia spoke up, "I was annoyed as all get-out with my husband shadowing me all the time until I realized Jack is afraid. He depends on me and can't even remember I'll be right back if I go into the bathroom. He's losing his memory, and I am his lifeline—his security. He sticks close because he is confused and afraid."

I have experienced some clingy dependence with my husband. The situation has improved lately as his health has improved, but he likes for me to be near all the time. When I have trouble remembering a name or am slow recalling a fact, I get peeved with myself. How strange and frightening the world must seem to a person who is losing memory and control because of disease, aging, or both.

A popular song written in 1927 includes these words:

> Me and my shadow strolling down the avenue. . . .
> All alone and feeling blue.

Those words describe the isolating situation caregivers experience with their clingy loved ones. As we turn to God for patience and strength, we discover God cares. Like the psalmist, our souls cling to God, and we find shelter and security in the shadow of God's wings.

## Prayer

Gracious God, I am frustrated with these annoying behaviors of my loved one

.........................................................................................

.........................................................................................

.........................................................................................

.........................................................................................

Enable me to offer patience and compassionate security for him/her as you do for me. Amen.

# THURSDAY
## *A Place to Scream*

**Read John 3:16; 5:24; 6:40; 20:31.**

Bob peered at me over his reading glasses as he talked about his pain. Suddenly he paused. Then, in a hushed voice of resigned desperation, he spoke, "I wish I could find a place to scream. I am so tired of being mature. I just want to scream." I was silent but my head and heart boomed, "Me too!"

What we were feeling in that moment has been expressed powerfully in a series of oil paintings by Norwegian artist Edvard Munch titled "The Scream." The sole figure, dressed in black, has a pear-shaped bald head, bulging eyes, gaping oval mouth, and hands with elongated fingers covering the ears. The agonized creature stands next to a fence. A sky streaked with blazing tongues of fire and blood makes a startling contrast with the backdrop of a bluish-black fjord. Munch's artistic capture of a tortured, superhuman, primal cry expresses what I'm sure many caregivers and care receivers feel when they wish to cut loose with a soul-baring, gut-wrenching scream.

There is comfort in knowing Jesus connects with this kind of human anguish and agony. He cried out in a loud voice from the cross, "My God, my God, why have you forsaken me?" (Matt. 27:46). A second time he cried out "with a loud voice and breathed his last" (Matt. 27:50). Jesus extends to his suffering disciples permission to cry out by example. There in the cries of Jesus, Bob and I are offered a refuge, a safe place to scream.

Praise God, the cross is not the end of the story. We manage to hang on because we know about Easter. The refuge Christ offers enables us and invites us to continue onward. There is the expectation of a better place with the risen Lord where the need to scream is forever erased. The Gospel of John is full of discourses in which Jesus develops the theme of eternal life to those who believe. The darkness, the despair, the deafening deadness are pierced by the promises: "For God so loved . . . ," "anyone who believes him who sent me has eternal life," "through believing you may have life in his name."

Even on the worst days, when, like the Munch subject, we want to cover our ears with long, thin fingers and scream, we hold on, trusting in the good news of God's merciful love.

## Prayer

Almighty, Everlasting God, this is a time when we are exhausted and afraid. I want to scream because

........................................................................................

........................................................................................

........................................................................................

Comfort your children who are care receivers and caregivers. Fill our hearts with the confidence and trust to believe in your plan of love and salvation. Amen.

# FRIDAY
## *Irish Eyes*

**Read Psalm 121.**

My husband has a happy habit of greeting me occasionally with "the song of the day." A favorite for us both is "When Irish Eyes Are Smiling." Bob playfully bats his enormous baby blues and sings with gusto, "And when Irish eyes are smiling, sure, they steal Nell's heart away."

This morning those eyes tugged at my heartstrings, but not in a lighthearted way. I was dashing off to an appointment with my spiritual director and popped into Bob's office to give him my customary good-bye kiss and to ask if he was wearing his med-alert button. The big Irishman sat slumped in his large black desk chair.

"Bob, what's wrong?"

"I knew you were busy getting off to your appointment, and I didn't want to bother you. I tried to button my shirt myself." He pointed to the mismatched buttons and buttonholes on the front of his red plaid shirt and held out his arms to show me the unbuttoned cuffs. He peered at me over the rims of his prism glasses and softly said, "I tried, but I couldn't do it."

I scurried to his side and thanked him for his efforts while I fixed the buttons. But I could not fix his sadness or the bewilderment at his inability to complete the task of dressing himself. The eyes were not smiling. They reflected helpless resignation. I tried to hide my own despondency with words of encouragement and love, but we both knew the truth about his deterioration and dependency.

Bob and I, care receiver and provider, experience profound loss from the relentless river of changes that runs through our days, months, and years. We also have discovered an unbounded source of aid—of strength, comfort, hope. Like the psalmist, we sing confidently that our help comes from the Lord, the maker of heaven and earth. Irish eyes twinkle; sometimes they cry. When they look to the Lord, they find the friend, the love, the joy that brings the lilt of Irish laughter to the deep recesses of the soul.

A wee chuckle bubbles up as I recall a favorite saying of Helen, sister to six younger brothers including my Bob. She enjoyed saying, "Never forget, Nell, that when Irish eyes are smiling, they are usually up to something." Oh, Helen, how I wish . . .

## Prayer

We turn our eyes to you, O Lord, in our weakness. We cannot in our own strength fix

but you help us when we look to you, O God our Father, in Jesus our Savior, and ask for the gift of the Holy Spirit. Amen.

# SATURDAY
## *A.M.A.*

### Read Psalm 13.

The phone startled me as I was deeply engrossed in research for a small "for hire" writing project. The deadline loomed, and I was taking advantage of the mornings Bob was away in the nursing center to make good progress on my work. I estimated eight more days to complete the job.

"Mrs. Noonan, this is the social worker at the nursing home. Your husband has decided he is leaving and going home today. He is adamant and doesn't care what anyone thinks. No one has been able to convince him he needs two to three more weeks of therapy. He has declared he is leaving even though it is A.M.A. [against medical advice]."

My first reaction was to deny that this was happening. Following the wave of shock, I felt an outburst of anger. I am not a skilled nurse, and Bob needs one around the clock. He is so weak he can't even get to the bathroom by himself. How would I manage? I was being treated for a compression fracture in my lower back from pushing him in a wheelchair up an incline. I had strict instructions not to lift or do even slightly strenuous physical activity.

The woman told me the nursing home would reluctantly discharge him rather than let him go A.M.A., so that he could continue to qualify for home health care through Medicare and to receive prescriptions from his doctor. Otherwise we were on our own. *O dear Lord, what am I going to do now?*

It had been years since I felt such intense anger. To

me, my husband's behavior seemed selfish, stupid, crazy, foolish, bullheaded, idiotic, brainless, absurd, dim-witted, irresponsible, insane. . . . My long pause probably had the case worker thinking I had fainted. I took a deep breath and told her, through clenched teeth, to tell him I would be there at 3:00 the next afternoon to bring him home.

I fell to my knees and cried out, "O Lord, how long? You know my strength is depleted. I simply can't do this. How in the world can I take care of him? How will I finish my project? I am so angry. O God, please."

Bob had his way; he came home. Somehow, with God's help, I managed to get through each new day. By staying up late at night, I even turned the project in on time.

## Prayer

O Lord, I am so angry and tired. Hear my cries: How long? How can I do this?

Really, God, don't you think this is enough already? Amen.

# SUNDAY
## *In a Rut*

**Read Exodus 14:26–15:3.**

Many Americans, like me, were raised in families that read the Bible and attended Sunday school. From early childhood to today, the Bible's stories of deliverance remain strong in our collective subconscious. The story of the liberation of the Israelites from Egyptian bondage continues to capture the imaginations of God's people. The interaction between Moses and the hard-hearted Pharaoh (and subsequent plagues) tantalizes and amuses those of us who know the good guys win in the end.

The tyrant holding Bob captive is chronic pain. He has a surgically installed drug pump and pills to deal with breakthrough pain. One day we sat in the orthopedic surgeon's exam room after another set of X-rays. We were told Bob's hip replacement was holding well. The source of his excruciating pain was not the hip. Bob grimaced and groaned as the doctor manipulated his leg. The doctor said he could do nothing more; the back and damaged sciatic nerves were the probable source of Bob's agony.

I dream of Bob's emancipation from chronic pain and misery. It's hard to keep spirits up, to carry on. Some days I crawl into a rut of numbed feelings, apathy, and pity for us both. I wear the same outfits, cook the same meals, and mindlessly play solitaire. In the recesses of my spirit I know the Lord is with me in my rut and will eventually fashion a glorious day of deliverance some time out there in our future.

Where I grew up in Mississippi, washboard roads and ruts were serious business. One sign posted on a country road warned, "Choose your rut carefully—you'll be in it for the next ten miles." We may be caregivers stuck in a funky rut. It may go on for ten miles or ten years, but the Eternal One invites us to the audacious hope that our holy work of service delights the God of deliverance.

## Prayer

Almighty Father, long ago you led a people from bondage, redeemed them, guided them to the Promised Land. I need to be delivered from my rut of

.................................................................................................................................

.................................................................................................................................

.................................................................................................................................

Come now and be with us. Amen.

## Sabbath Time

Write down some thoughts about your journey this week. What frustrations and feelings are making you cry to God? Where is God partnering you in your struggles? Did you receive God's gift of tears, mercy, or grace? Offer your reflections to the Lord.

.................................................................................................................................

.................................................................................................................................

.................................................................................................................................

.................................................................................................................................

.................................................................................................................................

.................................................................................................................................

.................................................................................................................................

# WEEK 2

Struggles with Identity

# MONDAY
## *Identity Crisis*

**Read John 10:1-5, 14-15.**

A key function of the human experience is pondering our identity: *Who am I? What gives me value? What is my relationship with others? Where do I fit? Am I good enough?* As the number of "senior moments" increases, the preponderant question shifts to *Who will I be when I can't remember who I am?* When memory departs and one's mental acuity diminishes because of Parkinson's disease, Alzheimer's disease, atherosclerosis, or aging, a profound sense of identity loss results. The experience can be frightening and often causes care receivers to develop a desperate clinginess. They need help with mental recall and constant reassurance they will not be abandoned.

At breakfast one morning Bob told me about a dream. He said, "I was lost. But I knew if I was picked up by the police, they would ask me where I was going. I would say, 'Where's Nell? She'll tell me.'" He abruptly ended the conversation and proceeded to enjoy his blueberry pancakes.

Later that morning I attended an Alzheimer's support group session. A sweet-faced lady with a halo of silver curls told us about a trip to visit her husband living in an Alzheimer's unit. When she entered his room, he asked, "Who are you?" She answered, "Marie." His response was, "That's my wife's name." Oh, the sadness of her identity crisis—a situation being repeated thousands of times every day when a loved one no longer remembers.

An e-mail from a friend related this scenario about a man in his eighties. He told a nurse at his doctor's appointment he needed to hurry because he had to go to the nursing home to eat breakfast with his wife. The nurse asked about his wife and learned she had Alzheimer's disease. When asked if she would be upset if he was late, he replied that she had not recognized him for five years. The nurse was surprised and asked, "And you still go every morning?" He smiled, patted the nurse's hand, and said, "She doesn't know me, but I still know who she is." That is true love. It is neither physical nor romantic. It is an acceptance of all that is, has been, will be, and will *not* be.

There is another love—that of the Good Shepherd. He leads us to green pastures and calls us by name. He lays down his life for his sheep and gives his wondrous, self-offering love, even if we can't remember who we are or who he is.

## Prayer

Good Shepherd, I recognize my true identity when

......................................................................................................

......................................................................................................

......................................................................................................

......................................................................................................

Help us care providers and receivers to remember, even when we can no longer remember, that we are loved, far more than we can ever imagine, today and always. Amen.

# TUESDAY
## *Friendship Pennies*

**Read Ecclesiastes 3:9-12.**

After my husband's hip replacement surgery, he went to a rehab facility for twelve days. The therapy was too strenuous for him, so he was sent to skilled nursing/rehab care. One of the four wings of the nursing home housed patients like Bob—people recovering from surgery, strokes, and so forth, who were expected to recover enough to return home. However, the majority of residents were there for long-term custodial care. They sat silently for hours in their wheelchairs staring into their laps or out into space. The staff affectionately referred to them as their "feeders" because they required assistance to eat (as well as with other physical needs).

The transfer between the two rehab facilities was done at suppertime, and we were immediately escorted into the dining room. Bob recoiled when he looked around and saw the expressionless faces of the "old folks." I asked the supervisor if there was a dining table where people were conversant, and she quickly assigned him to a table with three other men. When I left that evening, I felt troubled. Bob had made it painfully clear he did not want to be there.

During my visit the next day, I learned from Bob all four table companions had worked at the same aircraft company, in different engineering capacities, sometime during their careers. He excitedly told me one of the men collects Indian Head pennies. I was instructed to bring a particular roll of pennies from his collection for his new friend on my next visit. I breathed a sigh of relief. Bob was adjusting.

The friendships strengthened over time as the men talked about aging, life in retirement, and pennies. One evening I asked Bob about his friend's penny collection. He hesitated before replying: "This morning I asked Jim if I could look at his pennies and find out which ones he's missing so I could give him 'fillers' for his collection. He reached into his pocket and pulled out one of his penny pouches. I opened it and took a few out. They were wet. I told him the pennies were wet. And Jim said, 'I know. I peed on myself.'"

I tried to hide my smile as I asked, "What did you do then, Bob?"

"I handed them back and didn't say anything. I didn't want to embarrass him 'cause he's my friend."

## Prayer

Everlasting and Eternal God, thank you for friends sent to be companions on our journey, especially

........................................................................................................

........................................................................................................

........................................................................................................

I am grateful that regardless of the decline of our bodies and minds, we have the blessed assurance you will always be with us offering your pennies of enduring friendship and steadfast love. Amen.

# WEDNESDAY
## *Candy Apple Red*

**Read Isaiah 43:18-21.**

One of the stickiest problems when a loved one becomes incapacitated concerns driving and owning a car. To this day my husband, Bob, thinks he can drive, and a year ago convinced the clerk at the DMV office he needed his license renewed (incredible since he was sitting in a motorized wheelchair and couldn't stand for his photo). He doesn't drive; we won't let him. And that is that.

My friend went through a difficult situation with her mother who had been moved to a nursing home. Not only was Linda dealing with her own emotional grief, she was taking care of her mother's neglected household. There were car payments on a car her mother, Lorayne, would never be able to drive again, and expenses were mounting. Linda made the decision and told her mother she was going to sell her car.

The conversation went something like this: "Mom, you are not getting strong enough to drive your car again. My car is in good shape, and we need only one. I think we should sell your car and get rid of those payments."

"Oh, I need my car. I can drive. No, your idea is a bad one."

"Mom, when you get ready to drive again, you can always buy a new car. All my life you've told me you wanted a candy apple red car, and you've never had anything but black, white, or tan. How about when you get ready to buy another car, you buy your red dream car?"

Lorayne smiled at her clever daughter and nodded. "Okay."

The next week Linda sold the car.

At about the same time that the car sold, Lorayne had a stroke and went back into the hospital. The fragile octogenarian grew more and more frail. She couldn't talk, and the quality of her life diminished rapidly. Sadly, her time with us came to a quick close.

A good friend who knew about Lorayne's dream for a candy apple red car decided to grant her wish. Joe made a model car, painted it bright red, and placed it on the altar at the funeral. Linda and her friends smiled at the thought of Lorayne zipping around heaven with a blissful grin on her face and her Lord in the passenger seat.

Today Bob brought up his desire to drive again. I gave him a sharp, curt "No way." Then I remembered Linda's skillful example. We caregivers need to search for the "candy apple reds" that might soothe the losses our loved ones have to face.

## Prayer

Good and Gracious Lord, my care receiver has lost the ability to

.................................................................................................................................

.................................................................................................................................

.................................................................................................................................

Show me ways to dignify and respect all dreams in this life and beyond. Amen.

# THURSDAY
## *The Sky Is Blue*

**Read 1 Peter 1:3-9.**

A bumpy spell following Bob's two surgeries two weeks apart lasted five months. One day I began to realize how negative our words had become when people inquired about how we were doing. Our words were honest and understandable for our situation, but I am surprised folks didn't run the other way from our gloomy reports. Bless their hearts, they even seemed genuinely interested.

A change would be desirable. Bad news, sad news, suffering, and chaos do not have to determine who we are or what we say. As I reflected on answers people give when others inquire about their well-being, I recalled the incredible example a dear friend gave us.

In her fifties, "Carrie," a gifted poet, Christian educator, wife, and mother, was diagnosed with lung cancer. The petite, physically fit lady had always maintained a healthy diet and a vigorous exercise routine. Her prayer life and scripture study were equally robust. Discipleship and volunteerism filled her days. The disease came as a shock. She fought courageously for two years before crossing into her new life. I miss my friend, her poetry, our conversations about faith, and tasty slices of her freshly baked bread.

Carrie did something remarkable during her battle with cancer. When someone asked her how she was doing, she answered, "The sky is blue. God is good." No matter how excruciating the pain, the response was the same. I wish I had been given an opportunity to unpack in detail what she meant, but part of her essence as a poet was to use words to evoke feelings, new forms to draw us deeper into the mysteries of the Holy, and metaphors to connect the sacred and the secular. She was content to hold life loosely, to give it wings, to explore depths of existence. Through poetic words and gracious dying, Carrie fashioned creation out of chaos and suffering.

Her message was an instruction to hang in there with God in spite of pain and disappointments. She invited us to have faith, to trust, to live with eternity in view and spiritual ears tuned to the music of heaven. Carrie offered us a gift that crosses the boundary between this life and the life to come—the gift of hope. "God so loved the world that he gave his only Son, so that everyone who believes in him may not perish but may have eternal life" (John 3:16).

## Prayer

O God, I feel despair because

...................................................................................................................

...................................................................................................................

...................................................................................................................

Help me and my care receiver to be so filled with your love that we face the future strong in hope and confident in your "blue sky" goodness. Amen.

# FRIDAY
## *In My Distress*

**Read Psalm 107:4-9.**

Twenty-two children, ages five to eleven, in traditional African dress, ran down the aisles waving and shouting. Drummers started a rhythmic beat, and an unforgettable event began. The children sang, danced, and praised God with every ounce of their being. Joyful, youthful exuberance flowed from each supple body and each wondrous face.

The Hope for Africa Children's Choir was on a four-month tour of the United States, and our fortunate church was selected to be one of the performance sites. Humble United Methodist School, where the choir children reside, opened its doors in 2004 in Uganda to serve children from war-ravaged areas and those from homes affected by HIV/AIDS. *Humble* is an acronym for "Helping Ugandan Mwana by Loving Example." *Mwana* is the Lugandan word for *child*. Two hundred four pupils from nursery to seventh grade call the school home. The purpose of the tour is to advertise and encourage financial and prayer support for this ministry. The dream is to have more havens for vulnerable orphans and suffering children.

When the program concluded, the pastor asked the children, "What does Jesus mean to you?" One child said Jesus means bread when he is hungry. A shiny-faced boy beamed after telling us Jesus loves all the little children of the world and Jesus means he is loved. Several youngsters recited Bible verses, displaying their all-encompassing trust and faith in Christ Jesus.

Then a shy little slip of a girl, who looked to be eight or nine years old, raised her hand. The pastor repeated his question, "What does Jesus mean to you?" With a beautiful, lilting voice she told us her mother died birthing her. She had no home, no place to go. Then she came to the school where she now sings and dances with the others. "Like in the Bible, I cried to the Lord in my trouble, and he heard my cry and delivered me from my distress. That's what Jesus means to me." I looked over at Bob in his wheelchair at the end of the pew. He was teary-eyed, too, touched deeply by a child's simple sermon. That evening we were entertained by messengers straight from the heart of God.

## Prayer

Lord God, I cry out to you when

........................................................................................................

........................................................................................................

........................................................................................................

Lord of Dance and Song, your steadfast love for all children endures forever. You hear the cry of a child, *mwana,* in Uganda, and you hear us in our times of distress. Like the little African girl, may we trust you to deliver us. May we be bold enough to tell of your deeds with words of hope, songs of joy and, above all, loving example. Amen.

# SATURDAY
## *Good Friday*

**Read John 19:31-37.**

Three years had passed since my husband's last trip outside the Dallas/Fort Worth Metroplex when I mentioned how nice it would be to visit our son and his family in Arkansas over the Easter weekend. Never did I imagine he would want to try, but his response was not only positive, it was enthusiastic. We phoned Bobby, made motel reservations, and a few days later began the 350-mile trek from our home in North Texas.

Bob did well on the trip, and both of us enjoyed the sunny weather and lush springtime scenery. After checking into our room, we drove eight miles farther up a mountain road for a delightful family supper in our son's lovely home with its spectacular view. We knew he and his wife, a registered nurse, would be occupied with their busy medical clinic the next day but had expected the children would be out of school for Good Friday. However, the kids had to make up a snow day, which meant Bob and I were on our own Friday.

At breakfast in the motel the next morning we inquired if there was a short excursion we might take to enjoy the natural beauty. The gracious woman who fixed our plates of hot waffles told us about her favorite place—Haw Creek Falls high up in the nearby Ozarks. With our directions written on a paper napkin, we began our drive. To our amazement, we found the obscure turn that forded a creek and looped off into a remote campground. I discovered a path wide and firm enough to accommodate Bob's motorized chair. After some precarious teetering, Bob wheeled out onto a rocky shelf next to the waterfalls. We sat for a long time in silence as our thirsty spirits gulped in the sounds and sights of our natural surroundings.

Earlier in the day we had lamented the fact we would miss Good Friday church services—truly one of the most powerful worship experiences of the year. Determined to commemorate this significant holy day somewhere somehow, I had packed the Bible along with our snacks and drinks. Sitting on barren rock next to the wheelchair, I listened to Bob read aloud the Passion story found in the eighteenth and nineteenth chapters of the Gospel of John. He read slowly and deliberately, sometimes pausing with overwhelming emotion. I looked up into the face of my beloved, whose brow is marked by "crown of thorns" scars from three episodes in a metal halo. He loves his brother Jesus and identifies intensely with the Man of Suffering and Sorrow. Tears ran down our cheeks as the scriptural phrases reverberated throughout our outdoor cathedral with its background music of splashing waterfalls.

## Prayer

O Jesus, Lamb that was slain, keep me near the cross. I experience the cosmic dimensions of your wondrous self-offering love when I recall

..................................................................................................

..................................................................................................

..................................................................................................

I am overwhelmed with gratitude. Amen.

# SUNDAY
## *Namaste*

**Read: Genesis 1:26-27; Hebrews 13:1-2.**

Decades ago I read a story that still haunts me. While on a journey in the Himalayas, an American adventurer saw a crippled beggar child along the side of the road. She was beautiful, except for her thin, twisted legs. With sparkling, deep, velvety brown eyes, she looked up at the foreigner and smiled. Pressing her hands together in front of her chest, she bowed slightly and said, "*Namaste.*"

When the traveler asked the guide about the little girl and her salutation, he explained that in many families caught in poverty, the father breaks legs or otherwise maims a child, then designates her or him as an alms beggar in order to get income to support the family. This child with the bright smile showed no resentment for her lot in life. The American, humbled by the child's poverty and her humility, was amazed at her happy aliveness.

The child's greeting may simply have meant "I greet or salute you" or the respectful meaning "I bow to you." In recent times, the word *namaste* has come to be associated with yoga and spiritual meditation. Poetically, it means, "I honor the Spirit in you which is also in me."

I recalled the beggar story when the word *namaste* appeared in an account of the 1978 arrival of eleven refugees from the killing fields of Cambodia to a church-sponsored haven in the United States during bitterly cold weather. Clad in thin, pajama-like suits and flip-flops, the five adults and six children greeted their welcoming party.

With hands held together, thumbs at forehead, they bowed and said, "*Namaste.*" The Americans took off their coats, wrapped them around the refugees, and rushed them to warm, waiting cars and their new church family.

Our caregiving ministry teaches us spiritual mutuality—with the beggar child, Cambodian refugees, and one another. Each care provider, "made in the image of God," is called to cultivate honor and respect for the impaired care receiver, also "made in the image of God." Dear caregivers, I bow to you and whisper, "*Namaste.*"

## Prayer

Almighty and Eternal God of the Universe, teach us to salute the place of Highest Love and Spirit both within ourselves and within our loved ones. I do that when

........................................................................................................

........................................................................................................

Praise to you for the honor of being your child. Amen.

## Sabbath Time

Reflect on the stories this week about identity. Write down your thoughts on who you are, how you relate to others, and what gives value or purpose in your life. How do you relate to the Man of Suffering and Sorrow?

........................................................................................................

........................................................................................................

........................................................................................................

........................................................................................................

Thank God for God's love.

# WEEK 3

Struggles with Guilt

# MONDAY
## *Ungodly Thoughts*

**Read Ephesians 2:4-9.**

The e-mail startled me. Usually my communiqués are bits of family news, clever stories, alumni and church newsletters, and the like. This one originated through the contact page on the Web site for my books. The writer had received *Not Alone: Encouragement for Caregivers* as a Christmas gift. She is caring for her disabled, depressed mother and also a thirty-nine-year-old brother with cerebral palsy. "Jennie" is married and works full time.

After thanking me for writing such a "truthful book," she continued, "I have a question for you. It's a very delicate question, which terrorizes me to even think about, but I do not think it was covered in your beautiful work. The question is: Have you ever asked God to take your husband home? I have many times desired God would put an end to my poor mother's frustration and desperation. . . . Is it ungodly of me to have this thought? I would love your take on this."

I quickly determined the most helpful response was an honest one. Only a few days earlier, while in excruciating back pain, I had a recurrence of my "widow wish." That honest confession, shared months previously with my spiritual director, had prompted me to write a blatantly truthful devotion on that very subject. Like Jennie, several caregiver readers had told me the earlier book did not go deep enough into guilt and dark thoughts. They wished I would more fully address those issues in a sequel.

So, yes, dear Jennie, I admit I sometimes am scared by the periods of depression and darkness within myself. They may last for a few weeks but generally not more than a few days. Here am I, a writer about caregiving and the spiritual life, known as someone who loves God and wants to give hope to God's people. Jennie, all I can tell you is that my "widow wish" and your "orphan wish" may be ungodly thoughts in the sense that we want to tell God what to do, when to end the suffering. We are thoroughly human, and in us there is weakness when we want our will, our way, to control the world. We deceive ourselves if we think we are not sinful. We repeatedly miss the mark of pure, unfettered love that is God's vision for our relationships with others, ourselves, and the Creator.

But our hubris is only part of what we are. I look into my heart's mirror and see the soiled spots, but I also see a child created in the image of a God whose love, mercy, and grace cannot be contained. Even my selfish, small heart holds a capacity to seek forgiveness, to be cleansed from within. Caregivers, the gospel is good news. Believe it. We are forgiven and loved beyond measure.

## Prayer

O Merciful God, you know our darkest thoughts

.................................................................................................

.................................................................................................

.................................................................................................

We beseech you to enter our hearts. Uphold us and fill us with your grace, that we may know the healing power of your love. Amen.

# TUESDAY
## *Hungry*

**Read John 6:27-35.**

Two weeks earlier June could say "I love you" and blow kisses when I exited her nursing home room. Then she reached the point where she could mouth the words, whisper my name, and touch her lips. Two more days went by, and she was unresponsive. She already had told us she was no longer interested in eating, and eventually she shook her head at the offer of even sips of water. Her distraught daughter and I watched as the beautiful, intelligent woman turned into nothing more than a small pile of ninety-six-year-old bones.

It was excruciating to witness my sweet friend starve to death. Sitting by her bedside holding her hand, I found myself praying for her death. I pleaded with God and felt guilty. Several times in the weeks before she was too weak to speak, June asked me, "Why is it taking so long? I just want to go home." And then I would beg from the depths of my soul for the Lord to grant her wish. No sooner did the words form on my lips than a wave of guilt engulfed my troubled spirit. Frankly, I didn't care at that moment what God's will was. "Father God, she needs to die. Please take her home today." But more days went by. I rejoiced when the phone call finally came to tell me she was now "in a better place with Dad."

The vigil with my friend ushered in a painful awareness of the agonies of starvation. I sat helplessly watching June disappear and thinking about the enormity of hunger around the globe. I had read that 12.6 million American "children live in households where people have to skip meals or eat less to make ends meet."* When we look at global realities, more than 963 million people go hungry every day.

June's favorite book of the Bible was the Gospel of John. When her eyesight became poor and her hearing was seriously diminished, I would sit on her bed with her face right next to mine and read her requests. One of the last scriptures I "shouted" to her was the story of Jesus feeding the five thousand found in chapter 6. A few verses following the feeding account, Jesus spoke to his disciples: "I am the living bread that came down from heaven. Whoever eats of this bread will live forever." June's hunger for God was satisfied by her deep faith in a Lord who never fails to feed God's children with love, mercy, and extravagant amounts of grace.

## Prayer

Source of Life Eternal, Bread for the World, Redeemer of Souls, I hunger for

........................................................................................................

........................................................................................................

........................................................................................................

As we prepare meals for our care receivers, may we give thanks for your abundant supply to fill our needs. May we provide our loved ones generous servings of patience, compassion, and respect. Amen.

* *The United Methodist Reporter*, supplement to August 21, 2009, issue.

# WEDNESDAY
## *Killing Me*

**Read 1 John 1:5–2:2.**

It wasn't until we pulled into our usual handicapped parking space at church on the Sunday morning before Thanksgiving that I realized I had forgotten to load Bob's motorized wheelchair in the car. Not to be deterred from weekly worship, I dashed down the hill to the closet of emergency equipment and retrieved a large push wheelchair. Bob got safely transferred and off we went. After worship, we enjoyed coffee and fellowship with a number of loving friends. Sometimes discussion is about things theological, but more often we share what is happening in our lives, community, and nation. We are "family."

In order to return to our car, I had to push Bob, who weighs more than two hundred pounds, up a steep incline. About two-thirds of the way up, I leaned forward and pushed with all my might. Then it happened. Pain shot through my lower back. Somehow I managed to get us home and get meds and meals, but the ache intensified.

Tuesday I saw my doctor. She ordered X-rays and gave me a couple of prescriptions that my stomach could not tolerate. A day of nausea made me feel worse. Because of the holiday weekend, the radiology report did not come back for a week. I had a compression fracture and was referred to a neurosurgeon who referred me to a pain doctor who gave me another prescription and scheduled me for cortisone injections.

I had trouble sleeping, could not get comfortable for

even five minutes, and grew resentful with each restless toss. I had days then, and still do now, when I hate my role as my husband's caregiver. It is literally killing me physically and emotionally. I'm not surprised to read that caregiving, particularly over a period of several years, can actually reduce a caregiver's life expectancy.

Today, from the depths of my weary psyche, I uttered my "widow wish" and my longing to God for an end to our suffering. Some days everything seems to be closing in on me, and I wonder if I can handle one more day of caregiving responsibility. I feel terribly guilty at those moments when I wish my husband would die and leave me to find some normalcy in my senior years. I felt so selfish this morning. In anguish and pain, I prayed from deep within my spirit. On my knees I confessed my brokenness. Somehow comfort, forgiveness, and release washed over me. I was reminded again that God's grace is always big enough to love me and all wayward, hurting children unconditionally.

## Prayer

Lord God, we caregivers hurt; we sin. We hate the diminished quality of life for our loved ones and ourselves. Our situation stirs up feelings of

........................................................................................

........................................................................................

........................................................................................

You never leave us in the depths of despair. You come to us, loving Lord, with your seamless forgiveness and overflowing grace. Praises be to you, Most High. Amen.

# THURSDAY
## *Heavy Burdens*

**Read Matthew 11:28-30.**

"Guilt" was the theme for the Alzheimer's support group session. Caregivers carry around a heavy load of that nasty stuff. We feel guilty when we wrestle with feelings of anger and resentment about what is happening to our loved ones and ourselves. We magically think somehow, somewhere, sometime we can make our care receivers better. Not only are we burdened with the physical and emotional demands of caregiving, but we add unwarranted, irrational burdens of guilt when we can't provide care perfectly. We struggle with a contagious caregiver's disease a young woman in the support group has labeled "Careheimer's."

Today a lovely silver-haired lady commented, "It's hard to know what to do anymore. I feel like I've aged five years since my husband got lost last week. He went out to get the mail and couldn't find his way back, so he knocked on someone's window. She phoned the police. I try to let him do things, but now I am embarrassed and angry even though I know he can't change the way he is. Plus I feel locked up with him."

Jesse, whose wife was diagnosed with Alzheimer's disease fourteen years ago, said he feels real shame and guilt because of something he "never dreamed would happen." With sadness in his voice, he softly said, "I can't remember what she was like before."

Jesus said, "Come to me . . . and I will give you rest. Take my yoke upon you, and learn from me. . . . For my yoke is easy, and my burden is light." The words comfort and encourage us, especially on shaky days.

Jesus was a carpenter before he began his ministry of teaching, preaching, and healing. He probably made yokes. They may be designed for one animal only, but the most common ones have a wood beam with two U-shaped frames (oxbows) and a swivel in the center for attaching the tug pole of a wagon or plow. This type is designed for a pair—or team—of oxen, horses, or mules.

When Jesus says, "take my yoke," I picture him custom crafting one just for me. It fits perfectly, does not rub or pinch, and matches the contour of my neck precisely. Fashioned by strong, skillful hands and a loving awareness of what I need for the journey, my yoke is easy and comfortable.

Another miraculous part of my image involves the other ox in my pair. It is Jesus himself, helping me with the heavy burdens, encouraging me in my weariness, giving soul-rest through his companionship. He is indeed "gentle and humble in heart."

## Prayer

Lord Jesus, Nazarene Carpenter, I am wearied with my burdens of

.................................................................................

.................................................................................

.................................................................................

May I remember you are quietly present, with love and compassion for care providers and their care receivers. I am filled with gratitude for the way you help me make it through another day. Amen.

# FRIDAY
## *Arnold Palmer Syndrome*

**Read 2 Thessalonians 2:16-17; 3:16.**

An old joke (one of the few I can remember) goes something like this: Moses and Jesus were playing golf. They came to a long par-three hole that had to carry over water. Jesus teed up first and was addressing the ball when Moses asked, "What club are you using?"

"A five iron," Jesus answered.

"A five iron? You can't carry water with a five iron. You need more club."

"Arnie Palmer hits with a five iron here," Jesus said. Jesus swung and hit the ball about 165 yards. It splashed into the water.

"I'll get it," volunteered Moses. As he approached the water, it parted. Moses walked out like Charlton Heston, retrieved the ball, and walked back to the tee as the water filled in behind him.

Jesus teed up and was ready to swing when Moses asked, "What club are you using?"

Again Jesus said, "A five iron."

"A five iron? You need more club than that."

"Arnie Palmer hits with a five iron here," Jesus said as he hit the ball. It carried about 185 yards this time and splashed into the pond.

"Don't bother, Moses. I'll get it myself."

Jesus strolled down to the pond and calmly walked on the water to retrieve his ball.

Just at that moment, a foursome came up from behind

and saw Jesus walking on the water. They said to Moses, "Who does that dude think he is—Jesus Christ?"

"He is Jesus Christ," replied Moses. "But today he thinks he's Arnold Palmer."

I think I remember this joke because of its "get back in place" message with an unexpected reversal. It is not a situation where someone who is lesser goes on an ego trip and parades himself as someone greater. Instead, a greater someone insists on being less than he really is.

For six years my primary role has been caring for my chronically ill husband. Endless days of caregiving bring on anger and depression. I often yield to the temptation to equate who I am with being Bob's lackey, cook, laundress, nurse, maid, and dutiful wife. The little girl inside me wants to cry, "What about me?" Then I look at this good man with his misshapen body and suffering-strained face, and guilt floods my soul because of my self-centeredness.

But there is another me—a "real" little girl with a playful spirit; endowed with a calm heart and a peaceful core; a curious, creative creature. My task this day is to see that caregiving challenges and guilt feelings do not break in and spoil the inner sanctum where my true identity is God's beloved, graced child.

## Prayer

Lord God of Mercy and Grace, teach me to balance my role as care provider with the real me who is

.........................................................................................................

.........................................................................................................

.........................................................................................................

Amen.

# SATURDAY
## *Wrestling with Demons*

**Read Luke 11:14-26.**

There is a simple truth about caregiving—it tests you. It brings out the best and the worst in you. Personally, many days the emphasis appears to be on the worst. I am one of those caregivers on a path seemingly without end, filled with potholes of stress and puddles of guilt as I helplessly watch my husband deal with pain. Like other care providers, I often sacrifice personal needs to the primary goal of maintaining the well-being of my loved one.

We take on this role because we are compelled by the dictates of society and the mandates of our hearts. But here is the rub. There is a point in almost every day when I resent being Bob's caregiver. It's as though an inner demon takes over and stirs up the resentment smoldering underneath the hours of kindness and patience, just waiting to pounce and devour the love and peace in my heart. When I successfully stuff it, the anger turns inward. And because I can't openly be angry with Bob, who cannot help having a chronic illness, the anger manifests itself in "situational depression." It is a terrible cycle that goes on and on and on. We hit the sixth anniversary today of the time I left my job to be full-time care provider for my husband.

At times I totally accept this job—the servant ministry; the demon of resentment sleeps and takes vacations. God's present plan for my life brings abundant daily blessings. Most important, a deeper relationship with God is developing. More compassion for others has slowly increased. Honest, authentic sharing of self through my writing provides support to thousands of people who take care of someone with chronic illness or impairment. I praise God for the manifold gifts of this experience.

Nevertheless, the wrestling match with the demon of resentment continues to plague my inner spirit. The condition reminds me of a familiar Native American story: One evening an old man told his grandson about a battle between two wolves that goes on inside all people. "One is Evil. It is anger, envy, jealousy, sorrow, regret, greed, arrogance, self-pity, guilt, resentment, inferiority, lies, false pride, superiority and ego. The other is Good. It is joy, peace, love, hope, serenity, humility, kindness, benevolence, empathy, generosity, truth, compassion, and faith."

The grandson thought about his grandfather's words for a minute and then asked, "Which wolf wins?"

The old man simply replied, "The one you feed."

That lesson fits me well. I can't change my situation, but I can work on changing myself.

## Prayer

Enable me, Gracious Lord, to truthfully face my inner demons

and grant me the courage to battle against the wolf of

May the good wolf reside in my heart today and in the days to follow. Amen.

# SUNDAY
## *Guilty Feeling*

**Read John 1:14-17.**

Caregivers are prime candidates for what researchers call the toxic guilt trio: could have, would have, should have. No day goes by that I don't catch myself saying, "I feel guilty that I can't be the care provider I want to be." My conversations with other caregivers confirm "guilt tripping" as a common experience. The guilt feeling is like a knot in your gut taunting you: where will you fail next?

Last week an incident brought an explosion of guilt. My husband's pain pump has been maintained and replaced as needed over a span of twelve years. He always complains about pain, so I didn't think much about it when, a year or so ago, he heightened his litany about how much he hurt. The doctors already had performed a knee surgery and a total hip replacement, installed a larger pain pump, and then added a bolus machine. They increased Bob's dosages, but nothing eased the chronic pain.

Finally a wise nurse suggested a catheter dye test. It revealed a six-inch piece of tubing broken off and lodged next to the sciatic nervous system. I realized my husband had been tortured for Lord knows how many months. Since everyone thought he was getting narcotics through the pump, all resisted giving him the pills his broken body needed. Oh, God, how he suffered, and the pathos of realizing we could have eased his pain.

I wept over this discovery. Then I felt a wave of guilt slam me as if I were in turbulent surf, leaving me gasping for air and choking on gulps of foul salt water. I haven't stopped "should-ing" myself. I should have believed Bob when he said he needed another pain pill.

Well, guess what? Fretting about what happened won't change history. The simple truth is I didn't know. Guilt is hard to shake, but dwelling on the emotion is unhealthy. We caregivers need to ditch the idea we should be omniscient and know what is going to happen when and how. Such faulty thinking can foster a kind of guilt that sabotages mental and physical health. We lose patience, our tone of voice becomes strained, the house becomes dirty, we don't exercise, we eat too much or too little. Or we fail to give our loved one medication he or she needs to relieve pain.

## Prayer

God of Grace and Mercy, I feel guilty about

..................................................................................................

..................................................................................................

..................................................................................................

Allow me to bask in your unconditional love as I struggle to care for my loved one through another day. Amen.

## Sabbath Time

Write down any insights about this week's theme of guilt.

..................................................................................................

..................................................................................................

..................................................................................................

..................................................................................................

# WEEK 4

Struggles to Find Equilibrium

# MONDAY
## *Happy to Do It*

**Read Psalm 34:1-9.**

Prayer is the bedrock of my husband's daily existence. For him, prayer is not complicated but very simple. It is a conversation between his heart and God, where all his questions and all God's answers can find each other. Bob does not intellectualize about prayer. He humbly lets the Holy Spirit cool his anxiety, stir up his faith, and surface the deep longings of his heart. I don't know if it is the gift of gab from kissing the Blarney stone, but this old Irishman is never at a loss for words when it comes to prayer.

Morning, noon, and evening we pause, hold hands, bow our heads, and express our gratitude, praise, and petitions. Occasionally Bob lets me lead, but generally he likes to be the one to speak aloud to our Lord. This morning was one of those times when I listened quietly to his eloquent words:

"Good morning, God: Father, Son, and Holy Spirit. I love you. We love you very much. We adore you and praise you. God, I hurt so bad. Nell hurts too. But, Lord, we are happy to go through these problems if it improves our love for you. Amen."

Yes, Bob, you nailed it. The struggles, the challenges, the good things, and our ways of making meaning of our lives are purposeful if they bring our hearts closer to the heart of God.

With teary eyes, I turned to look out the window at the hanging basket of cheerful pansies and the feathered friends at the bird feeder. I studied the hand-painted Delft bowl, with a windmill scene on the side, filled with blooming paperwhites. At that moment, this environment, punctuated by Bob's words, made me feel safely sheltered within the presence of a good God.

"Happy are those who take refuge in the Lord" (Ps. 34:8b). "Happy are the pure in heart" (Matt. 5:8, GNT). The word *happy* is often interchanged with *blessed* in the holy scriptures. It is not about happiness in the secular sense, but the word is derived from a right relationship with God. That is what Bob meant when he said, "We are happy to go through these problems." We are not enjoying the difficulties and pain, but we accept them in the hope they will lead us to the blessing of a closer, improved relationship with the Lord we love.

## Prayer

Lord God, I thank you for the gift of prayer and for your loving provisions of

..............................................................................................................

..............................................................................................................

..............................................................................................................

Assist me in discovering and rejoicing in the blessings of my caregiving pilgrimage so that I may be a blessing to you, my care receiver, and others. Amen.

# TUESDAY
## *Helping Hands*

**Read Exodus 17:8-13.**

The book of Exodus is packed with one adventure story after another occurring during the Israelites' forty-year trek from Egypt to the Promised Land. The scripture I chose for today is one that came to mind when I reflected on what two amazing friends do for me and Bob.

Moses and the Hebrew people journeyed into the wilderness and came to Rephidim, a camping place without enough drinkable water. Moses struck a rock as the Lord instructed him and out poured water needed for survival. The camp of this ragged band caught the attention of the Amalekites, living in an area the Israelites would have to cross to enter Canaan. When Moses became aware of this impending raid, he told his field commander, Joshua, to gather troops and fight them. Moses took his brother, Aaron, and a man named Hur with him to a hill where he could oversee the action. His raised arms symbolized the Lord's power and inspired troop morale. But his arms grew heavy and his two companions had to hold them up until the battle was won.

Others are often needed to assist in times of caregiving crises. My husband had two major surgeries within two weeks. The total hip replacement would require several days in a hospital twenty miles from home. When two dear friends heard about it, they made the unbelievable offer to keep our six-year-old sheltie with them while Bob was in the hospital. I had planned to board her, but Nancy and Dick would not hear of it. The evening before the early-morning surgery a well-groomed Molly, her sleeping crate, and paraphernalia were deposited with the two remarkable seniors.

Six days later, after Bob had been moved to a local rehabilitation center, I went to get Miss Molly. I learned that on the first morning Dick had taken his boarder for an early walk. Back at the open front door, he unfastened her leash. Before he could close the door, Molly turned and took off down the street. Dick, in loafers, ran after her. Nancy, still in bathrobe, quickly changed and followed in the car. Three blocks later, Dick, panting and exasperated, saw the dog and shouted, "Molly, sit." Miraculously she did. They welcomed the car ride back home.

Sometimes I imagine myself in a wilderness, battling to stay the course to eternal life. Like Moses, my arms (and heart, mind, and spirit) grow weary. I also have two steadfast, generous friends to hold me up. They board our dog, fix my birthday lunch, bring food, phone, make hospital visits, and the list goes on. Nancy and Dick are my Aaron and Hur, but I bet it was easier to hold up arms than to keep a feisty, furry boarder.

## Prayer

God and Protector of Sojourners, I feel weary when

.............................................................................................................

.............................................................................................................

Thank you for

.............................................................................................................

who generously bless us with support. Amen.

# WEDNESDAY
## *Sunday Visitor*

**Read Matthew 9:32-35.**

Bob spent six weeks in hospital and rehab facilities following hip replacement surgery. One of his major worries was that his little dog, Molly, might forget him. I asked and was enthusiastically granted permission to bring her for a visit.

There were physical therapy sessions during the week, and my writers' guild meets on Saturday so we chose Sunday afternoons for Molly's visits. I took the little sheltie rescue dog to the groomer during the week. When the Sabbath arrived, I added a small baggie of treats, a plastic bowl, and a bottle of water to the canvas bag holding a package of clean laundry and a couple of get-well cards for Bob.

Six-year-old Molly slipped into her best manners for the visits. The attention-getter pranced and danced down the wide hallways and right into the room where Bob sat with open arms. When we exited the room to go out to the courtyard to let Molly run, a woman appeared in the door right across the hall. She exclaimed, "I know that dog. That's Molly. I'm her groomer." Another happy reunion took place as we learned the woman's mother was in rehab following knee replacement surgery.

A few days later, Bob was moved to a different facility where his roommate was recovering from a severe stroke. My heart ached for Joe as he struggled to speak, eat, walk, do anything for himself. He spent hours sitting in his recliner staring out the window. His television was on, but he rarely looked at it. Surprisingly, I could sometimes figure out what he was trying to say or what assistance he needed in spite of his garbled words.

Molly came to the new facility for her next Sunday visit with Bob. When she entered the room, Joe's face lit up as he reached to pet the friendly, furry stranger. He spoke the word *dog*. Over and over, loud and clear, with perfect pronunciation: "dog, dog, dog." We joyfully laughed together over the small spontaneous miracle of healing. Joe made daily progress in his speech after that. His family placed a framed picture of his dog on his bedside table. He would smile, point, and tell everyone who entered the room, "My dog, my dog."

The Gospels are full of recorded events when Jesus had compassion for and healed the sick and infirm. I often puzzle how he did those miracles, how he enabled the mute to speak and the lame to walk. Such incredibly marvelous deeds—and he didn't even have a little dog to assist him.

## Prayer

Great Healer and Friend, thank you for coming during disorienting times of pain and sickness when

.............................................................................................................

.............................................................................................................

.............................................................................................................

You enable us to regain our equilibrium when you

.............................................................................................................

Glory and praises be to you this day and forevermore. Amen.

# THURSDAY
## *Day by Day, The Jesus Prayer*

**Read 2 Corinthians 1:3-7.**

A retired high school journalism teacher belongs to my writers' group. He issued a challenge after I read at a recent session. He commented, "You write that you cope *day by day*. I want to know, and I think your readers would benefit, if you tell us more about how you do that." Caregiving is so individualized and subjective, I would never try to tell anyone how to do it. But I did agree to share a few personal coping techniques.

A major aid I use over and over during the day is the Jesus Prayer. I have known and recited it for so many years I cannot remember when the simple little prayer became bedrock to my daily existence. The roots of the prayer go back to Paul's letter to the Thessalonians when he says "pray without ceasing" (1 Thess. 5:17). Its elements are found in the early church life of the first disciples. By the sixth century it emerged as a developed doctrine and teaching in the Christian devotional system.

This is the Jesus Prayer:

Lord Jesus Christ, Son of the living God,
Have mercy on me, a sinner.

I use a breathing rhythm as I recite: inhaling or taking in "Jesus air" on the first line and exhaling or letting out bad thoughts and inner toxins as I repeat the second phrase. The breathing and the words calm both body and mind. Because the prayer is intensely Christ-centered, the rhythmic repetition effects a shift in focus from stress and fear to Jesus and self-offering love.

About five o'clock on Bob's first day back home, after thirty-six days in the hospital, I noticed he was slumped over and quite still in his recliner. He was difficult to rouse and seemed confused. His blood-sugar levels had been difficult to control since his surgery, and his symptoms suggested the problem could be glucose-related.

As I went for the glucometer, I began to repeat the Jesus Prayer softly. Bob was lethargic, but I managed to get a reading—a dangerously low forty-three! I placed a glucose tablet in his mouth and urged him to chew. That was followed by a glass of orange juice. Forty minutes later I took another reading—still forty-three! What to do? Call 9-1-1? The words rolled out, "Lord Jesus Christ, have mercy."

After I spoon-fed Bob some supper, which took another forty minutes because he was so sluggish, the reading was fifty-seven. I knew we had turned the tide and he would probably be okay one more time.

## Prayer

Beloved Son of God, you are a stabilizing, comforting influence as near and life-giving as our very breath. I am aware of your merciful presence when

.....................................................................................................

.....................................................................................................

.....................................................................................................

Thank you. Amen.

# FRIDAY
## *Day by Day, Everlasting Arms*

**Read Psalm 91.**

Often I am asked, "How do you do it?" One valuable tool I employ is the regimen of reading scripture and devotional books and praying each morning. That practice undergirds my day. The beginning time varies because I first take care of Bob's meds and breakfast and wait for him to get settled with nap, crosswords, or coins. At night I follow a routine also. Because weariness dictates its length, it may be as short as a recitation of the Twenty-third Psalm and the Lord's Prayer.

Two or three times weekly I use a brief order of worship called Compline, found in the small, well-worn Episcopal Book of Common Prayer on my bedside table. The English word *compline* is derived from the Latin *completa*, meaning complete, and by extension, completion of the day. The service includes some scriptures, and I am especially fond of Psalm 91, a comforting assurance of God's protection. Another part of the service that connects with the deep recesses of my being is the canticle (scriptural song) of Simeon based on Luke 2:25-35.

During the many years I served as a church educator, I saw that children loved this story. They helped set up the homemade props: a small wooden box with portals and columns to represent the Temple; raffia figures of Joseph, Anna, Simeon, and Mary holding eight-day-old Jesus, and a tiny basket with a pair of tiny white birds.

I remember their rapt faces as I told about a devout old man, Simeon, who had a revelation that he would not die until he saw the Messiah. Guided by the Holy Spirit, he went one particular day to the Temple. When Mary and Joseph approached with Jesus and their offering of two turtledoves, Simeon took the baby in his arms. He praised God and sang, "Master, now you are dismissing your servant in peace, according to your word; for my eyes have seen your salvation" (Luke 2:29-30). The joy we share at the news of the Christ child's entry into history returns to me every time I hear those words.

Compline closes with words of benediction, but right after I turn out the light, there is one addition to my ritual. I recite a passage of scripture learned in Miss Olson's second-grade Sunday school class: "The eternal God is thy refuge, and underneath are the everlasting arms" (Deut. 33:27, KJV). In my mind I crawl into those arms to be cradled until I fall asleep.

Days are unpredictable and demanding. Morning devotions and Compline are stabilizing routines that help me get through—day by day.

## Prayer

Thank you for the joy and peace I felt today when

.......................................................................................................................

.......................................................................................................................

"Guide us waking, O Lord, and guard us sleeping; that awake we may watch with Christ, and asleep we may rest in peace" (Book of Common Prayer, 135). Amen.

# SATURDAY
## *Day by Day, Church Family*

**Read Galatians 6:2, 10; Philippians 2:4-5.**

A source of great encouragement for my caregiving journey is my church. Bob and I attend the 8:15 morning service, and my soul is like a sponge soaking in every minute of prayer, scripture, sermon, and music. Oh, yes, the music—especially the music—by and for a community of worshipers with its power to massage and transport me to a place of grace-filled bliss. Within that space, my croaking voice unites with piano, organ, bells, the lovely and the not-so-lovely voices of the church family to make glorious music of praise and thanksgiving to a gracious God. Why anyone would miss out on that kind of Sunday morning experience is hard for me to understand.

When Bob was in rehab at the nursing home, I found solace and fellowship with my church family. One week I told our Sunday school class I planned to go from there to a later morning service offered at Bob's facility, so we could worship together as was our weekly habit. When I wheeled Bob out of his room, I looked up the hallway and saw Connye and Jim, two members of our class. "We wanted to worship with Bob too." A warm feeling of Christian love and support lifted our spirits.

Residents in wheelchairs or on walkers gathered in the dining room. The service was led by a lay mission chaplain. Connye and I served those who wanted, or whose diet allowed, donuts and coffee, hot chocolate, or tea. More than a few frail-looking elders held up two fingers to signal they wanted two donuts!

The "congregation" sang enthusiastically to the taped music and listened quietly to the "teaching." After a short prayer, the service ended abruptly, but I could tell the residents wanted more. I summoned Connye, who has a lovely voice and is an experienced worship leader, to lead us in "Jesus Loves Me" and the Lord's Prayer. She not only responded to my summons but also asked if the congregants had other favorites. One octogenarian eagerly requested "In the Garden." When the song was over, he asked Connye if she knew what God's name is. She began a list: God, Jesus, Lord, Savior, Yahweh, Redeemer. The man interrupted, "God's name is Andy. Andy walks with me, Andy talks with me." Everyone got a good chuckle over his playful interpretation of the chorus words.

Worship in any format nurtures and sustains me, but I have a special gratitude for congregational worship, which feeds not only on Sunday but remains in my memory to comfort and strengthen me day by day all week long.

## Prayer

Lord God of Grace, Mercy, and Music, we, your children, regardless of condition of body and mind, have a primary purpose to worship. When I worship you, individually or in my faith community, the experience brings

Amen.

# SUNDAY
## *Day by Day, Silence*

**Read Psalm 62:5-8.**

A workshop at a Christian educators' conference decades ago permanently changed my life. There I received a prayer tool based on a book by Basil Pennington, *Centering Prayer*. The session offered suggestions for overcoming problems that discourage people from praying. We learned how to relax for prayer, how to listen for God's words, how to handle pain and distractions that hinder our attempts at achieving deep communication with the Other. Effective prayer is not always simple, and my copy of the book is well worn from the many times I have returned for reminders on the practice of "centering."

Over the years several silent retreats nurtured my desire for inner silence. The goal of my present personalized style is fifteen to twenty minutes a day when I take three deep breaths, relax, and turn off my mind. I select a word or phrase such as "Jesus," "Lord God," or "*Maranatha*" (Come, Lord) to help me let go of distractions and to focus. If distractions nag, I write them down so I can dismiss them, and then repeat my word.

Some days the exterior noises and demands make it impossible to quiet interiorly. But when a quiet mind does open a space, it fills with God's presence. The experience inches me toward kindness, gentleness, patience, trust, and the peace that passes understanding. My puddles of silence can be anywhere, including hospitals, doctors' offices, home, in cars, and on planes. This form of prayer has taught me prayer is not a project but a process.

For me the key is to empty—to relax, relax, and relax some more—in mind, emotions, and body. The movement I seek is to bring the mind down into the heart. The payoff is a kinder, more patient care provider—for at least a while.

A wall plaque hanging in our den features this quote from nineteenth-century essayist and poet Ralph Waldo Emerson: *Let us be silent that we may hear the whisper of God.* Yes, let the silence begin so we caregivers may hear the gentle call to bring our burdens to the Lord, who will gift us with rest from our weariness, mercy for our inadequacies, and unbounded love for our bruised spirits.

## Prayer

You never turn away from us, Lord. We are not alone. Speak to me, Lord; your servant is listening. I hear

.....................................................................................

.....................................................................................

.....................................................................................

Amen.

## Sabbath Time

Reflect on the ways you restore equilibrium when disoriented or exhausted. Were there any insights this week? How do you plan to take better care of yourself?

.....................................................................................

.....................................................................................

.....................................................................................

# CONCLUSION

Caregivers are heroes filled with devotion and compassion. However, they are notorious for neglecting their own physical, mental, and emotional needs. Another important but overlooked component for their health is spiritual well-being. This twenty-eight-days workbook invited you to carve out time and space to nurture your spiritual side. I hope you found the experience beneficial enough to want to continue a daily devotional session.

Within God-times, we allow our breaking hearts and weary souls to meet God at the deepest level of our suffering and struggle. When that occurs, a wondrous thing happens: God consoles and strengthens as only God can. A second outcome is surprising and humbling: we learn to console others in the ways God consoled us.

You may wish to repeat this twenty-eight-day cycle of prayer, reviewing your notes and journaling new thoughts and feelings. You may decide to use other devotional guides. Whatever you do, I pray you will continue to pay attention to your spiritual health.

God cares about your wholeness and loves you more than you can imagine. Daily, invite the Lord to partner you on your caregiving journey.

May blessings of grace and peace be yours in abundance,
Nell Noonan

# REFLECTION QUESTIONS

These questions are designed to stimulate further reflection for individuals or to be used by small discussion groups. Each week has a theme. I suggest you review an entire week before reflecting on the questions.

## Week 1: Struggles with Frustration and Faith

1. What frustration or annoyance got to you this week? How have you handled it? How might you move forward?

2. What do you control in your life? What guarantees does being a Christian bring to you? How does your relationship with God affect your caregiving?

3. What peeves you most about your care receiver? How do you cope with frustrations?

4. Do you ever feel God is absent from your life? How do you respond ? When do you sense God's presence?

5. Think about what delights you most about your care receiver. What losses tug at your heart?

6. Recall a time of anger and frustration with your care receiver. Why did you react so strongly? What insight might you gain as you look back at that experience?

7. How is your faith in God challenged by your caregiving journey? Where do you find strength to go on?

## Week 2: Struggles with Identity

1. Who do you say you are? Do you hide your private self? Is it scary or freeing to dig around honestly in your heart and soul?

2. Who do you think people say you are? Who did the people think Jesus was? Can you identify with Jesus' experience when people did not understand who he really was? Explain.

3. What feelings arise when you face memory loss or confusion either in your care receiver or yourself? How is your faith helpful or unhelpful in the situation?

4. When you are deep in despair, what gives you the courage to carry on?

5. When it feels like the bottom has fallen out, what sources of hope can you turn to?

6. How do you identify with the Man of Suffering and Sorrow? Think about how the Passion story can inform who you are and what you do.

7. How does knowing we are "made in the image of God" affect your relationship with your care receiver? with others in the world who are alike or different? with yourself and with God: Father, Son, and Spirit?

## Week 3: Struggles with Guilt

1. Some caregiving days are a living hell when we are stretched beyond belief. What "ungodly thoughts" do you have? Do they make you feel guilty? How?

2. What differences do you see between warranted and unwarranted guilt? How do you deal with either form?

3. How might you deal with any issues of unresolved guilt? What is your experience of confession and reconciliation of a penitent?

4. Where is your source(s) of help when you face heavy burdens of care responsibilities plus guilt for not being a "perfect" care provider?

5. Think of ways to find a healthy balance between your

needs and those of your care receiver. What will you do to take care of yourself?

6. We all struggle with inner demons and need healing. What is your biggest challenge?

7. Guilt and shame can poison our caregiving ministry. How can they be recognized? What is the role of grace in your life?

## Week 4: Struggles to Find Equilibrium

1. What role does prayer play in your life? What kinds of prayer work for you? Name benefits you experience when you pray.

2. Where do you find support for your caregiving ministry? Are you feeling isolated? Do you ever push help away? How might you learn to receive the support others offer?

3. Disorientation often accompanies caregiving and illness. Have you found sources to aid you in regaining your equilibrium? If not, think about where you could turn for assistance.

4. In what situations during this week were you aware of God's presence?

5. Where were you able to find joy this week?

6. Do worship and music play a stabilizing role for you or your care receiver? If these are helpful, consider ways to incorporate music in your caregiving environment.

7. Consider including times of silence in your days, simply experiencing God's presence. If this is already a practice for you, what did you hear this week in God's whispers? How has your image of God changed over time? Has your image of yourself changed as you have cared for your loved one?